South Pacific Islanders

The islands of the South Pacific were populated by people from Southeast Asia, beginning about 50,000 years ago. They were left to themselves until the sixteenth century, when European countries began exploring the area, opening it up to the Western world and the inevitable clash in cultures and values. In the nineteenth century, many of the larger islands were colonized by European nations who built schools and taught islanders Western ways in the mistaken belief that these would make them better people. Independence and self-government in this century has sparked a cultural revival on many of the islands, and attempts are being made to recapture many of the customs suppressed by years of foreign domination. Vilsoni Hereniko is a Fijian who advises on teaching English in Fiji. A member of the Fiji Arts Council, he has written poems, plays, short stories and a book on Pacific art. Born in Britain, Patricia Hereniko is an editor with the Institute of Pacific Studies in Suva, Fiji.

Original Peoples

SOUTH PACIFIC ISLANDERS

Vilsoni & Patricia Hereniko

Rourke Publications, Inc.
Vero Beach, FL 32964

Original Peoples

Eskimos — The Inuit of the Arctic
Aborigines of Australia
Plains Indians of North America
South Pacific Islanders
Indians of the Andes
Zulus of Southern Africa

Frontispiece *A beautiful palm-fringed bay on the island of Bora Bora.*

First published in the
United States in 1987 by
Rourke Publications, Inc.
Vero Beach, FL 32964

Text © 1987 Rourke Publications, Inc.

Library of Congress Cataloging-in-Publication Data

Hereniko, Vilsoni.
  South Pacific islanders.

  (Original peoples)
  Bibliography: p.
  Includes index.
  Summary: Describes the origins, history, and culture of the native people inhabiting the South Pacific islands and examines the impact of Western influences and the problems facing them today. Includes a glossary of terms.
  1. Oceania — Juvenile literature. 2. Oceania — Social life and customs — Juvenile literature. [1. Oceania] I. Hereniko, Patricia. II. Title. III. Series.
  DU18.H47 1987 990 87-4332
  ISBN 0-086625-259-2

Photoset by Direct Image Photosetting
Printed in Italy by G. Canale & C.S.p.A., Turin

Contents

Introduction

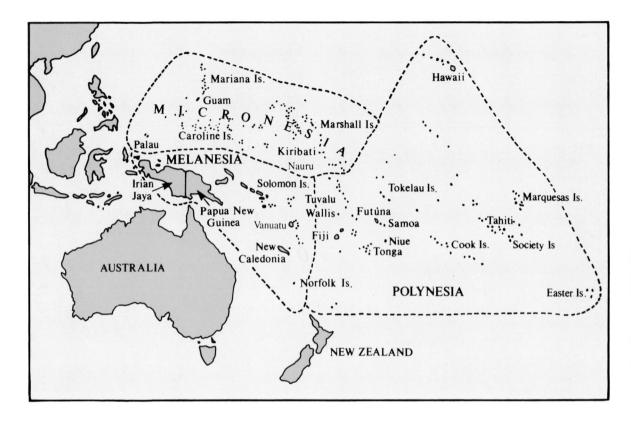

The Pacific — the "peaceful" ocean — stretches from the Arctic Circle in the north to Antarctica in the south and, despite the name, can rage destructively from time to time with cyclones, hurricanes, tidal waves, electrical storms and many other extreme weather conditions. It is an area of the world where the earth's solid surface appears above the water only as scattered islands, some low and made of coral, others high and of volcanic origin.

On these islands are to be found peoples, and cultures of great variety, and thousands of different local languages. These differences, and the ocean itself, make communication difficult between Pacific peoples. However, certain island groups share certain common characteristics.

The Micronesian islands (the U.S. Trust Territory, Kiribati and Nauru) are located in the North Pacific; the Melanesian islands (Papa New Guinea, Solomon Islands, Vanuatu and New Caledonia) in the West Pacific; and the Polynesian islands lie in the South Pacific. The Polynesian triangle runs south from Hawaii to the northern tip of New Zealand, bulging a little to include

Fiji, and over to Easter Island at its easternmost point.

The following pages describe something of Pacific life, particularly on three of the larger Polynesian islands: Fiji, Tonga and Western

Many Pacific islands are flat and made of coral, the remains of tiny sea creatures.

Samoa. The Polynesians are a strikingly beautiful people. Like many other peoples in the world today, they must learn to manage the inevitable conflicts that arise as their traditional ways come face to face with modern ways and their own culture meets Western culture.

Chapter 1 **Historical Origins**

Migrations

Where do the islanders come from? What do they look like? We shall try to answer these questions in this chapter.

Many theories have been put forward by scholars who do not always agree with each other. The theory that is most widely accepted today is that the Pacific was populated by people from Southeast Asia, about 50,000 years ago. From Indonesia, these first migrants moved to New Guinea and Australia. Later migrants spread eastward to the Solomon Islands, Vanuatu and New Caledonia. Micronesia was probably populated direct from Southeast Asia.

About 3,500 years ago these migrants reached Fiji. Soon afterward the spread continued to the Marquesas, Tonga, Samoa, Tahiti, Hawaii, the Cook Islands, New Zealand and the rest of Polynesia.

Thor Heyerdahl believed that the people of the Pacific were originally from South America, since the sweet potato of South America became an important food plant in the Pacific,

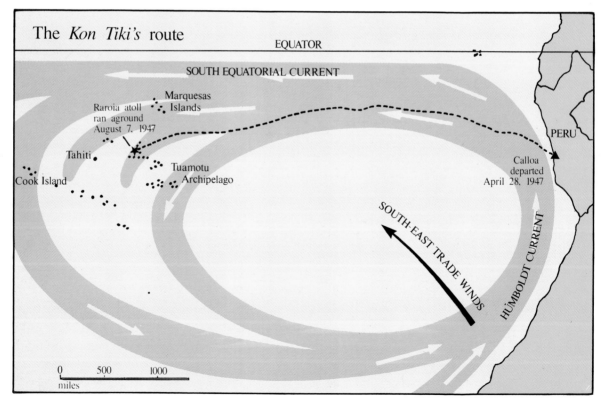

The *Kon Tiki's* route

EQUATOR

SOUTH EQUATORIAL CURRENT

Marquesas Islands

Raroia atoll ran aground August 7, 1947

Tahiti

Cook Island

Tuamotu Archipelago

PERU

Calloa departed April 28, 1947

SOUTH-EAST TRADE WINDS

HUMBOLDT CURRENT

0   500   1000
miles

especially to the Maoris of New Zealand. In 1947 he set out from Peru on a raft-like canoe built in the style believed to have been used by the early migrants. He wanted to see where the currents and the wind would take him. His raft *Kon Tiki* landed on a reef east of Tahiti. To-day, most people believe that, although people from South America did reach the island in the

The raft Kon Tiki *en route from Peru to the Raroia atoll, east of Tahiti.*

eastern Pacific, their influence was late and not very important.

Apart from the broad pattern of migration outlined above, there have been thousands of smaller movements and countermovements in various directions, throughout the history of the Pacific.

Polynesia

You can tell where an islander comes from by the way he or she looks. As a group, the Melanesians are usually dark-skinned, of medium height and have fuzzy hair. In fact, their general appearance is very similar to the Aborigines of Australia or the Bantu of Africa. The Micronesians tend to be of similar height with brown skin rather oriental eyes and straight black hair. In contrast, the Polynesians are usally taller, have lighter skin and straight black hair.

The native Fijians are regarded as having the bodies of Melanesians but the culture of Polynesians. Considerable influence from Tonga, especially on the smaller islands to the east, meant that Polynesian traits transferred to the culture and also, to a certain extent, to the physical appearance of present-day Fijians.

In the Western world, Polynesia is better known for the scenic beauty of some of its islands, its elegant cultures with their liberal views on love and freedom, and its beautiful women. This was perhaps why Gauguin, the famous French painter, was drawn to Tahiti, and why Robert Louis Stevenson, the author of *Treasure Island* and other books, chose to live in Samoa.

Left to right: a Polynesian boy, a Micronesian girl and a Melanesian boy.

Scenes such as this lured the French painter Gauguin and the British author Robert Louis Stevenson to the South Seas.

11

Chapter 2 **Pacific Lifestyles**

Beliefs

We shall try to reconstruct life in the South Pacific before the period of sustained European contact, which began in the eighteenth century. Many features of the old way of life can still be found, especially in remote villages and isolated islands.

Pacific islanders believed in invisible gods of the universe, as well as in the spirits of dead ancestors and other kinsmen. The spirits were supposed to have considerable power for good and for evil, so it was best to do what pleased them. Tonga and Samoa placed great importance on the god Tangaroa who was believed to grant favors to faithful followers.

Chiefs were believed to have a lot of *mana*, or spiritual powers, and the

Tradition has it that a bargain struck with a spirit-god gave the people of Beqa, Fiji, the ability to walk on white-hot stones.

The funeral hut of a dead Tahitian chief — powerful even in death.

more powerful the chief had been in real life, the more he was to be feared and revered in death — when it was believed that he acquired supernatural powers. (Fijians also believed that a person's *mana* could be transmitted to another). Tribal wars were widespread then and cannibalism practiced. Disputes were usually over land, fought against other tribes or invading foreigners from another island group.

There were sacred places, which were *tapu* (forbidden) and had to be avoided. Misfortune fell upon those who broke such laws. Some of these places still exist today. As in the Christian religion, the islanders also believed in life after death.

The supernatural was often blamed for accidents, illnesses and other misfortunes. Certain individuals had extraordinary powers to cure illness or to cast spells on their enemies. The ability to walk on fire was believed to be a gift from the world of invisible spirits. Today, Fijian firewalking is a popular attraction for tourists.

13

Survival

Fiji consists of more than 300 islands. Tonga has about sixty and Western Samoa has four. On the small atolls with thin coral soils, resources are very scarce. Therefore the majority of the people live on the larger islands.

The islands are surrounded by the sea, so fish was a regular item of the family meal. Shellfish, crabs, sea-slugs, octopus, turtle and other sea creatures supplemented the diet. Breadfruit, yams, *taro, kumara* (two kinds of vegetables) and bananas were the main crops. Later the islanders domesticated chickens, pigs, cattle, goats, dogs and horses.

Food was placed in the *lovo,* or *umu,* a kind of earthen oven filled with hot stones. All the family's food requirements for a number of meals were then covered with leaves and soil and left for an hour or so to cook. In this way, more time could be spent on other activities.

The seasons change little, and the islands are blessed with sunshine and rain all year round. Orange and guava trees grow wild on the fertile soil of the larger islands. Sweet-smelling flowers grow in abundance. Some of these plants are used for

Preparing a lovo, *complete with piglet and* taro.

making body oil and garlands, while others are very effective cures for illnesses.

The hibiscus in a wide variety of colors grows on all Pacific islands. So does the extremely useful coconut tree. Its leaves are used for thatch and baskets, the trunk for timber and its coconuts for drinking and eating. The cream of the flesh is a

A Tahitian war canoe.

favorite ingredient in cooking.

Sometimes there are hurricanes or droughts and they can do tremendous damage, especially on the coral atolls. People have been known to tie themselves to coconut trees to avoid being blown or washed away.

15

Social Organization

Polynesians kept their genealogies so that their family could be traced to a common ancestor, perhaps the leader of an expedition that colonized a whole group of islands. The power of a chief and his social status depended upon his connections.

Chiefs and family elders were highly respected and their advice sought and listened to. There were no old people's homes and each family was expected to look after the aged.

The extended family was the rule in the islands. One's family consisted of parents, brothers, sisters, aunties, uncles, cousins, nephews, nieces, grandparents, in-laws and so on. Families were large (ten or more) and often lived under the same roof. All members were expected to work together for the welfare of the *ainga,* or the whole family group.

A child had many "mothers" and "fathers" and was never lonely. It was common practice for grandmothers to adopt and raise grandchildren as their own. The children were usually

A group of Tongan people wearing fine mats — traditional dress to attend a wedding.

Typical Fijian houses, called bures. The chief's house will be the largest.

spoiled through overindulgence.

Marriages were arranged then, without consulting the couple. In most cases, such marriages were intended to strengthen ties between families or political bonds between tribes and clans.

Land was usually owned by clans or extended families, and worked by individuals. Ownership changed mainly by inheritance or warfare.

The roles of both men and women were clearly defined from an early age, and children learned by observing their elders. Males were expected to provide and protect, while females did the household chores and reared the children.

Shared Values

Sharing possessions and giving gifts were central to the islander's way of life. If someone was in need, people always gave generously, safe in the knowledge that others would be there to help them in times of need.

During important occasions giving gifts was magnified to a large scale. In Fiji, these exchanges of food and possessions used to be always accompanied by the presentation of whales' teeth. Finely woven mats in Samoa and beautifully designed yards of *tapa* in Tonga are the symbols of wealth and generosity. The dignified *yaqona* ceremony, in which a potent drink — made from the root of the *kava* plant — is shared, was another important feature of such occasions.

Islanders lived for the present. "Enjoy life now, for the future will take care of itself" was their motto. There were no clocks or watches, no cars or trains to catch, and no appointments to keep. The community did not frown upon what is considered today to be time-wasting. When it was not necessary to work, people sang and danced, or

A group of nineteenth-century Tongan men at a traditional kava-*drinking ceremony.*

A Polynesian extended family enjoying a meal laid out on banana leaves.

sat around the wooden bowl drinking *yaqona* and telling stories.

Houses had no wall partitions and neighbors were always welcome. People sat on the floor to eat, the men cross-legged while the women tucked their legs beneath them. Fatness was a sign of plenty. People never worried about their waistlines!

Island leaders today often refer to the above customs and values as "the Pacific Way." Many Pacific islanders think that the values of the past are obstacles to progress in the modern world and should be discarded.

#475

Fun and Games

Children were expected to help adults when called upon, otherwise they were left to do as they pleased. Adults did not expect them to participate in family discussions or to be around when the elders gathered, so children had a lot of time to play.

Celebrations of one kind or another were always favorite times for children. They could meet their friends and play their favorite games or indulge in mischief of one kind or another.

There were games that were played

An age-old pastime on the islands — swinging from trees.

by the boys only and others that were known as girls' games. The popular games for the boys were wrestling, dart-throwing and top-spinning. Nowadays they also play marbles and fly kites. Favorite games for the girls were juggling, cat's cradle and hopscotch.

Hide-and-seek was a popular game played by both boys and girls on moonlit nights. Sometimes, especially during festivals, boys and girls would gather on the beach where there would be much singing dancing, and merrymaking.

Because the sea was so close to the villages, swimming and other water

How many rowers are there in this Samoan longboat?

sports such as diving, floating on logs and swinging from trees were (and still are) common pastimes for the young-at-heart.

In the evenings, the elders of the village would gather the children around a warm fire and tell them myths and legends or fairy tales. Sometimes they made children recite nursery rhymes or sing lullabies. They also told them stories about the past. In this way memories were handed down from one generation to the next.

Chapter 3 **Pacific Art**

Things of Beauty

Our knowledge of what island art was like at the time of the first European contacts is gained through the pieces of art that are stored in museums around the world, as well as from texts and drawings in books.

Below *Making baskets from tree leaves.*

Above *A young boy being tattooed.*

There are, of course, many art forms that are still being practiced today, and they help us to imagine what it must have been like then. Raw materials were simple, and the islanders relied mainly on stone, wood, shell, coconut fiber and *pandanus,* a kind of plant.

Weaving was women's work. From the leaves of the *pandanus* plant, a wide variety of mats, baskets, hats and fans were woven. The women also made *tapa* for

religious purposes or for clothing.

Building the family *fale* or *bure* rested mainly on the men. The shape and structure of the houses differed between islands, although all used wood for the frame and thatch (from leaves or reeds) for the roof. Instead of nails, dyed *sinnet*, a hairy string made from coconut husks, held the wooden beams in place. Objects made for domestic use included canoes, coconut graters, wooden headrests, bowls, clubs and spears. Many of these had intricate patterns

A woman in Western Samoa making tapas.

or figures carved on them.

Oratory and tattooing were regarded as art forms. The young man who could speak well was greatly admired, so was the Samoan man with beautiful patterns carved on his body — usually on the face, buttocks and thighs. Fijian religion also required women to be tattooed about the groin and sometimes on the thighs and hips.

Music and Dance

The return of a loved one, the birth of a child, or the appointment of a new chief were occasions for celebration. New songs were composed to record the event and dances enacted to capture the spirit of the gathering.

Most dances were performed either sitting or standing. The men's dances, which were vigorous and energetic, included slapping the body, stamping the feet, twirling wooden clubs or spears in the air and imitating mock battles. The women's dances involved graceful head and body movements that illustrated the songs.

Grass skirts and headdresses add color to the tamure *dance of Tahiti.*

Dancers greeting Captain Cook during one of his voyages in the South Pacific.

Well known dances include the Fijian *vakamalolo*, performed by the women wearing colorful headdresses, the *tauólunga* of Tonga, performed by a female accompanied by two or more men, and the breathtaking fire dance of Samoa.

Costumes varied according to the type of dance and were usually made of leaves and sweet-smelling flowers. Feathers, fine mats, grass skirts and headdresses were worn in some dances. Musical instruments included bamboo flutes, shell trumpets, pan-pipes and slit drums.

The best known of Polynesian dances is the Tahitian *tamure*. The women revolve their hips in a very fast circular movement while the men open and close their knees in a scissors movement at a frantic pace. This particularly lively dance was banned by the missionaries, but it has recently been revived.

Chapter 4 **Outside Influences**

Explorers and Traders

Europeans began exploring in the South Seas in the sixteenth century. Portuguese and Spanish sailors, like Magellan in 1521, came in search of spices and wealth to please royal patrons, naming many islands on their way after their kings, queens and saints. They came from the east, first through the stormy southerly passage of Cape Horn, then later from Mexico.

Next came the Dutch, British and French. The famous mutineers of HMS *Bounty* searched in 1789-90 for a safe haven from the revenge of Captain Bligh. Captain Cook's scientific quest was for a "southern continent," and later for a Northwest Passage.

The colonization of Australia opened up new trade routes to China, another to join the American fur trade, yet another to India for sugar, rum and cotton. Ships stopped at Fiji for sweet-scented sandalwood, and *bêche-de-mer* (sea-slug). Polynesian lagoons yielded pearl shell and much seafood that, along with breadfruit and coconuts, provided valuable fresh food.

Captain James Cook (1728-79) made three long voyages in the Pacific and Antarctic Oceans. This map shows the route of his second voyage.

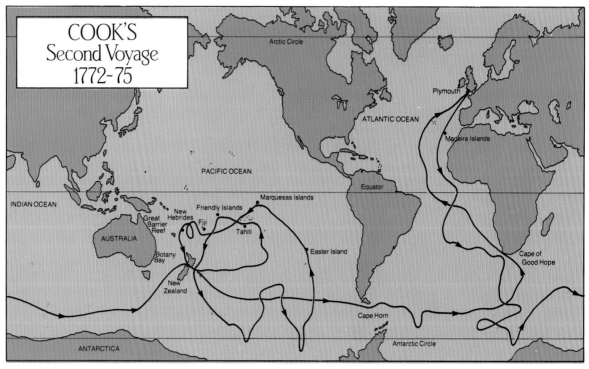

Captain Bligh and some of his crew being cast adrift by mutineers.

In the early nineteenth century, American whaling ships were responsible for discovering and recording most of the hundreds of Pacific islands, although European governments had already claimed some — the British claiming most because they monopolized mapmaking! Throughout this time, sailors were settling on the islands.

The South Pacific islanders had made contact with the outside world — its guns, sailing ships, commerce and much more.

Missionaries

European sailors of the sixteenth century had royal instructions to spread Christianity. Missionaries came three centuries later, often meeting with danger and difficulty. Some fell sick; most found it hard to learn the local languages; and one or two were even killed or eaten, because cannibalism was practiced in those days. However, some local chiefs welcomed them, because to "have" a missionary gave a chief glory above other chiefs, and also meant that European traders were more likely to visit.

These preachers were greatly helped in their work by their Pacific islander converts, first Tahitians and later Tongans. In Tonga, a Methodist, John Thomas, gained the confidence of Chief Taufa'ahau, who later became the king of all Tonga, George Tupou I. Many thousands were baptized following the example of their chief and Tonga has held the Methodist Church sacred ever since.

News of the church in Tonga reached Samoa, which also became Christian. Methodists, Congregationalists and Catholics were in constant competition for church members. People were instructed to dress moderately, go to church, and marry only one wife, so Samoan culture changed.

In Fiji, missionaries relied on help from local converts, especially

A human sacrifice being prepared in front of Captain Cook and some of his crew.

Flamboyant hairstyles like these were discouraged by the missionaries.

powerful chiefs like Varani and Cakobau, and Tongan friends. European churchmen created a Fijian alphabet, dictionary and grammar to translate the Scriptures and teach the local people. Gradually warlike ways died out, along with cannibalism. So did the following: flamboyant hairstyles and face painting, tattooing, earlobe piercing, the wearing of loincloths by the men and brief *liku* skirts by the women. A new kind of dress evolved — a *sulu* (a piece of cloth wrapped around the waist) and shirt for the men and a dress over a long *sulu* for the women. This missionary influence is still apparent today.

The Colonial Experience

Each island had its own unique culture, centuries old and passed from generation to generation by word of mouth. When the Europeans arrived, they found people who lived very differently from themselves.

Traders established plantations and harbors and gradually began to influence local people. They encouraged them to grow food for export to Europe and, where they would not, the foreigners brought in shiploads of plantation workers from elsewhere. Today, as a result, there are more Indians living in Fiji than there are Fijians.

Missionary teachings about the one true God toppled old beliefs in the spirits of ancestors and nature gods. Tribal wars were rife in the

A colonial administrator trying to settle a dispute over land between villagers.

The British flag being raised in Fiji in 1874 to symbolize Fijian chief's submission to British rule.

islands, especially Fiji, and the missionaries began to persuade their home countries to annex the islands hoping that this would restore peace.

Britain annexed Fiji in 1874. Samoa became a German colony in 1899 but was later administered by New Zealand. Tonga mainly ran its own affairs, although in 1900 it signed a Friendship Treaty with Britain and was given Protectorate status.

Being ruled by foreigners undermined the confidence of the islanders. They came to think that European things were superior, and that many aspects of their own cultures were barbaric, sinful and shameful. The colonial experience made the islanders suspicious of the *papalagi*, as they called Europeans.

Schools were built and European culture, history, language and religion were taught. Islanders were forbidden to speak their own languages at school. Instead, they were taught foreign ways, in the belief that these would make them better people.

31

Independence

The presence of foreign powers helped to restore stability in the islands before the Second World War. Some form of centralized government was established, medical services improved (resulting in increased population) and the islanders were taught to read and write.

In the 1960s and 1970s, Britain showed a keen interest in granting independence to her colonies and in withdrawing from the Pacific. France, on the other hand, continued to maintain a firm hold on her col-onies — New Caledonia and French Polynesia especially. Western Samoa became independent in 1962, Tonga and Fiji in 1970, the Solomon Islands in 1978, Kiribati in 1979 and Vanuatu in 1980. Cook Islands and Niue are self-governing. American Samoa is still under colonial government, although there has been talk of a future reunification with Western Samoa.

Tonga is the only kingdom in the Pacific, Fiji is a democratic Dominion, while Samoa is a state that allows only its chiefs to vote or be elected to power. Unlike the islands

The Royal Palace in Nuku'alofa, Tonga.

King Poulaho of Tonga in his ceremonial headdress of feathers.

of Melanesia, in Polynesia heredity mainly determines who will be leaders. However, there are signs that the people would prefer a more democratic system so that others who are capable, but are not of a chiefly family, can stand a better chance. Fiji's Prime Minister, Ratu Sir Kamisese Mara, is a good example of a chief who also commands the democratic respect and support of people at home and abroad.

Independence and self-government resulted in a cultural revival as nations fought for a national identity. Attempts are now being made to recapture many customs and art forms that had been suppressed by foreigners.

Towns and Cities

Towns grew up in convenient places, usually near good harbors and productive agricultural areas. The location depended also on suitability for governing the colony.

Fiji had a more varied economy than most Pacific islands. Both sugar towns and gold-mining towns developed.

Village people have envied town life. They see opportunities for education and employment, exciting stores and cinemas, and better medical and housing facilities. So, many villagers migrate to towns for a better life, giving rise to problems both in the towns and back in their own villages.

In towns, overcrowding occurs and poverty begins because the newcomers have neither the education nor the work skills suited to urban needs. They are farmers, not businessmen, teachers, doctors, or

Women are left to run farms when the young men leave their villages.

34

mechanics. They have come without money, which is not essential in the village. Yet one cannot live long in a town without money or a job. Some people work hard and manage to fit in; others are disappointed.

In the villages, farming suffers because generally it is the young strong men who leave. The old, the women and the very young remain to

Towns have grown up near good harbors and productive farming lands.

take care of everything. Social life and agricultural work cannot thrive when the backbone of the village community is gone, and governments are seriously trying to remedy the situation.

35

Tourism

Tourism to the wealthy South Seas visitor, is "getting away from it all" to enjoy the sun, sea, and relaxation. Tourism, to the Pacific islander, is an opportunity to improve his standard of living with the money that the tourist will spend.

Local people bring their food,

Villagers selling their wares to tourists.

dancing and handicrafts to the luxury hotels and to the wharves where the cruise ships dock. Their war dances and carved gods, clubs and spears really represent how islanders lived a hundred years ago, not how they live now, but the visitors prefer to think that the islands are still "untouched by civilization"!

Though poor in money, islanders are rich in their warmheartedness. One imaginative Tongan, Osika (Oscar), has turned his love of laughter and people to good advantage. Visitors are treated at his 'Oholei beach to swims in the warm lagoon, to local stories in an ancient cave by candlelight, and to abundant local food specialities and entertainment.

Tonga, Samoa and Fiji deal with tourism differently. Tonga would encourage tourism but scenically has little to offer. Samoa, though beautiful and well-supplied by international air routes, is afraid that the influence of foreign visitors will change the Samoan way of life too much, so tourism is restricted. Fiji is on international air routes and counts tourism as its largest industry, after sugar. It places great importance on the development of luxury resorts and tourist attractions.

Apart from tourism, the islanders' main sources of income are copra (made from coconuts), sugar (in the case of Fiji) and money sent by relatives living in New Zealand, Australia and the United States.

Tourism is restricted on some islands, but on others luxury resorts and tourist attractions are encouraged.

Chapter 5 **The Pacific Today**

Cooperation

The South Pacific islanders share similar problems and aspirations. They are aware of the challenges before them and are anxious to find solutions.

The 1960s and 1970s saw the emergence of regional organizations. Today there are more than 200 operating in the Pacific. These small islands with few resources and small populations realized that joining together would be to their advantage, giving them more bargaining power and better safeguarding their interests against foreign exploitation.

One of the most successful regional institutions is the University of the South Pacific, which opened in 1968. Many of its graduates are now leaders of their own countries.

Pacific islanders feel that they understand each other because of

A new hall of residence at the University of the South Pacific.

Some competitors at a recent South Pacific Games.

similarities in many aspects of their cultures and their past colonial experiences. Today, with the availability of sea and air travel, as well as telecommunication systems, contact and movement from island to island is more frequent than ever before.

Rugby, soccer and netball are very popular sports in the islands and indoor basketball, hockey, volleyball and tennis are also played. Inter-island competitions are organized either informally between sporting bodies or officially at the national level. Every four years, the South Pacific Games are held, where men and women from both larger and smaller islands compete. Goodwill and understanding are promoted, although, as at sports events elsewhere in the world, ill-feelings and jealousy are sometimes evident.

Regionalism and nationalism do not always go hand in hand, and occasionally there are signs of tension and dissatisfaction with the distribution of benefits resulting from regional projects.

Challenges

Perhaps the most important challenges facing the islands involve maintaining good relations both within the South Pacific and internationally, with countries that give development aid. These issues are complex and must be handled sensitively by island leaders.

The islands, although constitutionally independent, have become more and more dependent on foreign aid for their development. How can dependency be reduced? How can more profitable exports be found? And how can more local industries be established?

Education systems are modeled very closely on New Zealand's system and island students take the New Zealand School Certificate and University Entrance examinations. The islanders want to teach subjects relevant to local needs, but are hampered by limited resources and expertise.

There is rising unemployment, especially in Fiji. How can jobs be found for graduates and those who

Fijian schoolboys weaving with green coconut leaves — a traditional art.

Some Tongan teenagers gather for a drinking session. The one in the chair is pounding kava; *the other two are drinking beer.*

drop out of school? Today's teenagers have difficulty coming to terms with the contrasting expectations of their local culture and the imported sophisticated Western culture. Television is available in Samoa, and in Fiji video sets have become almost an essential item in urban households. The preferences of many youngsters are certainly changing, and many are confused by the clash of cultures, being unsure whether to remain South Pacific islanders or be "Westernized."

Fiji, unlike Tonga and Samoa, is a multiracial society and has the unique challenge of maintaining harmony between Indians and Fijians, whose cultures are vastly different — not to mention the Chinese, Europeans and other Pacific islanders who are also its citizens.

41

New Art Forms

In recent years, attempts have been made to revive those art forms in danger of being lost. Many islands now hold their own cultural festivals, and every four years there is a South Pacific Festival of Arts, bringing together all the island countries of the South Pacific.

Since many of the islands became self-governing, islanders have started to express themselves in new forms, by writing poems, short stories, plays and novels. Some of these writings are now being taught in schools.

Parliament House (the Fono*) in Apia has the traditional shape of the Samoan* fale.

Perhaps the most well known of these new artists who are using a language that is not their mother-tongue is Albert Wendt, a Samoan who has written a collection of short stories, a collection of poetry and three novels.

The developement of creative writing is important because, for the first time, islanders are expressing their own views about the past and their identity. These writings, considered together with those of foreigners, present a more complete and truthful picture of life in the

A colorful modern tapestry by Aloi Pilioko.

South Pacific.

Some artists, who carve or produce artifacts, are now experimenting with new materials and styles, but still trying to maintain a distinctly Pacific quality in their creations. A good example is Aloi Pilioko from Wallis Island, now living in Vanuatu. His tapestries are very popular and they continue to reflect inspiration from both Melanesian and Polynesian scenes and faces.

43

The Future

The South Pacific islands are keen on developing their own national identities. Samoa is even thinking of establishing its own national university to encourage Samoan culture and language. But there is a case for regionalism, for the islands acting together in world affairs so that they have more influence than each island would have if it spoke out separately.

The islands are seeking to improve living standards so that modern household items become available to the average family. Development, with foreign aid, means new roads, schools, hospitals, training centers, airstrips, water and electrical systems; recently computers have been introduced into Fiji's schools.

Two Samoans preparing copra, an important export.

Planes of Air Pacific keep islands, separated by miles of ocean, in touch.

Tourism is a big and expanding income earner for many island governments and people. But such development is not wanted at the expense of losing the islands' cultures. Leaders are concerned that children should be taught and be proud to speak in their mother tongues, as well as learning the international language, English.

Islanders are growing in confidence as they master the skills of the modern world, as they succeed in running their own businesses, schools and hospitals, and as more and more of their fellow-countrymen become lawyers, doctors, pilots and cabinet ministers.

The South Pacific islands now realize that they cannot remain indifferent to world affairs simply because they are relatively small, remote and unimportant at the international level. Their future is linked with the rest of the world. Today, they want to trade with the big giants and have joined forces with the European Economic Community (EEC). They seek more sports contacts with overseas countries and, above all, they want their voice to be heard in shaping their own destinies.

Glossary

Artifact Something made by a person, such as pottery; usually applies to something found at archaeological excavations.

Atoll A circular coral reef or string of coral islands surrounding a lagoon.

Cannibal A person who eats human flesh.

Copra The dried white flesh of a coconut, which can be used for making coconut oil.

Domesticate To tame animals that have been used to living in the wild and are unaccustomed to humans.

Extended family A family unit made up of three or more generations, either living under one roof or very near each other.

Flamboyant Something that is brightly colored or a person who behaves showily.

Garland A chain of flowers or leaves worn around the neck.

Genealogies Charts, or "family trees," showing the relationships and descent of an individual or his family over hundreds of years.

Kinsman A blood relative or a relative by marriage.

Liberal Broadminded; open to a wide range of opinions about matters.

Migration Moving from one country or region to settle in another.

Missionary A person sent to a country to convert its inhabitants to a particular religion.

Mutineers Soldiers, sailors or pilots in the armed forces who rebel against their officers.

Oratory The art of public speaking.

Supernatural Things that have no logical explanation.

Glossary of South Pacific Words

Ainga An extended family.

Bure Fijian word for house.

Fale A Samoan house.

Kava A ceremonial drink that is very strong.

Kumara A sweet potato.

Liku A very short skirt made from bark cloth.

Mana The spiritual power within a person.

Pandanus Screw pine plant.

Papalagi Polynesian term for Europeans.

Sinnet A thick string made from the fiber of coconut husks.

Sulu A simple piece of cloth wrapped and tucked around the waist.

Tapa Traditional cloth made from the bark of trees.

Tapu Something that is sacred or forbidden.

Taro A root vegetable about the size of a turnip.

Tauólunga A dance performed by a woman (or women) accompanied by two men.

Vakamalolo A dance performed sitting down; colorful headdresses are worn for it.

Yaqona The Fijian name for **Kava** (see above).

© Copyright 1985 by Wayland (Publishers) Limited
61 Western Road, Hove, East Sussex BN3 1JD, England

Books to Read

Some of the books listed here may no longer be in print but should still be available in libraries.

Let's Visit Fiji by John Ball and Chris Fairclough (Burke, 1985).

The Polynesian Triangle by Erick Berry and Herbert Best (Funk and Wagnalls, 1968).

Backbone of the King by Marcia Brown (University of Hawaii Press, 1984).

Kon-Tiki by Thor Heyerdahl (Rand McNally, 1984).

Let's Visit the Pacific Islands by Garry Lyle (Burke, 1984).

Hawaiians: An Island People by Helen G. Pratt (C.E. Tuttle, 1963).

The Fijian Way of Life by Asesela Ravuvu (Institute of Pacific Studies of the University of the South Pacific, 1983).

Inoke Sails the South Seas by Ronald Rose (Harcourt, 1966).

In the South Seas by Robert Louis Stevenson (University of Hawaii Press, 1971).

Samoa: A Hundred Years Ago and Long Before by George Turner (Institute of Pacific Studies of the University of the South Pacific, 1984).

Path of the Ocean: Traditional Poetry of Polynesia (University of Hawaii Press, 1982).

Acknowledgments

The illustrations in this book were supplied by the following: Camerapix Hutchison Library 21, 22 (top), 34; 22 left (William E. Townsend Jr.), 23 (Melinda Berge), 35 (Nicholas Devore) — all from Bruce Coleman Limited; Fiji Ministry of Information 39; Fiji Museum 29, 30, 31; Vilsoni Hereniko 10, 14, 16, 17, 19, 20, 24, 32, 36, 40, 42, 43, 44, 45; Kon Tiki Museum 9; National Maritime Museum 15, 27; University of the South Pacific 38; Wayland Picture Library 13, 18, 25, 28, 33; ZEFA *cover*, 7, 11, 12, 37. The author and publishers would also like to thank the following for their help: Steve Lucas, Randy Thaman, Kim Gravelle, and Michael Ogden. The maps on pages 6, 8 and 26 were drawn by Malcolm S. Walker.

Index